# USING RANDOMNESS TO TRADE FX CURRENCY PAIRS

*A SIMPLE WAY TO GET INTO FOREX TRADING | FX TRADING MADE SIMPLE | SECOND JOB WITH CURRENCY TRADING | RANDOMNESS*

*PAUL ARDENNES*

reviews and certain other non-commercial uses permitted by copyright law.

This book was published thanks to free support and training from:

The Wall Street Investors' Club

# Contents

# CHAPTER 1. INTRODUCTION TO RANDOMNESS

Forex traders use all sort of tools to try to gain an advantage over other traders. They will use fundamentals, algorithmic forex trading, technical indicators, wisdom, point and figures, pendulum and so on. Yet, a simple technique to get into forex trading is actually to use complete randomness and let the market tell us the direction to trade. If we use a well diversified portfolio, with enough currencies, the trading should be profitable. This system uses this view point. We use it at the club with reasonable success.

We aim at reaching 10% profit per month. With our sophisticated online calculator, we know exactly the number of lots we need in order to manage our trades.

The system is so simple that it requires only a bit of patience to wait for the currencies to tell us the direction. We use a robot for the exit, based on our target to reach 10% monthly or double our capital yearly. And we use a calculator for the risk management.

We use 2 platforms for this strategy. One experimental and one for the trading itself. All is explained in the Udemy course.

# CHAPTER 2. OUTLINE OF THE COURSE

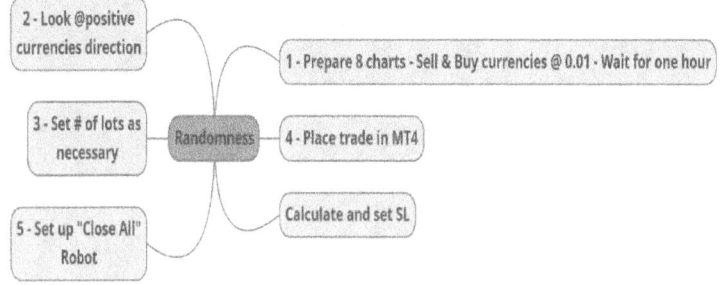

2 - Look @positive currencies direction

3 - Set # of lots as necessary

5 - Set up "Close All" Robot

Randomness

1 - Prepare 8 charts - Sell & Buy currencies @ 0.01 - Wait for one hour

4 - Place trade in MT4

Calculate and set SL

For note taking

# Chapter 3. Disclaimer

## RISKS ASSOCIATED WITH FOREX TRADING

Trading foreign currencies can be a challenging and potentially profitable opportunity for investors. However, before deciding to participate in the Forex market, you should carefully consider your investment objectives, level of experience, and risk appetite. ***Most importantly, do not invest money you cannot afford to lose.***

There is considerable exposure to risk in any foreign exchange transaction. Any transaction involving currencies involves risks including, but not limited to, the potential for changing political and/or economic conditions that may substantially affect the price or liquidity of a currency. Investments in foreign exchange speculation may also be susceptible to sharp rises and falls as the relevant market values fluctuate. The leveraged nature of Forex trading means that any market movement will have an equally proportional effect on your deposited funds. This may work against you as well as for you. Not only may investors get back less than they invested, but in the case of higher risk strategies, investors may lose the entirety of their investment. It is for this reason that when speculating in such markets it is advisable to use only risk capital.

## Risk Disclaimer for Forex Trading

Trading foreign exchange on margin carries a high level of risk, and may not be suitable for all investors. Past performance is not indicative of future results. The high degree of leverage can work against you as well as for you. Before deciding to invest in foreign exchange you should carefully consider your investment objectives, level of experience, and risk appetite. The possibility exists that you could sustain a loss of some or all of your initial investment and therefore you should not invest money that you cannot afford to lose. You should be aware of all the risks associated with foreign exchange trading, and seek advice from an independent financial advisor if you have any doubts.

**Benefits and Risks of Leverage**

Leverage allows traders the ability to enter into a position worth many times the account value with a relatively small amount of money. This leverage can work with you as well as against you. Even though the Forex market offers traders the ability to use a high degree of leverage, trading with high leverage may increase the losses suffered. Please use caution when using leverage in trading or investing.

Hypothetical Results Disclaimer

THE RESULTS FOUND ON THIS WEBSITE ARE BASED ON SIMULATED OR HYPOTHETICAL

For notes taking

# CHAPTER 4. RANDOMNESS SET UP

In this lesson, we will setup our experimental platform to trade 8 charts. This setup will give us the direction that we want to use on our trading platform as explained in the next lesson. We will choose AUDCAD, CADCHF, EURJPY, GBPCHF, AUDCHF, EURAUD, EURUSD, GBPNZD

Here is a picture of how it will all look

| Order | Time | Type | Size | Symbol | Price | S/L | T/P | Price | Commission | Swap | Pref |
|---|---|---|---|---|---|---|---|---|---|---|---|
| 50450011 | 2019.06.13 18:26:14 | sell | 0.01 | audcad_ecn | 0.91190 | 0.00000 | 0.00000 | 0.95116 | -0.10 | -0.13 | -4.21 |
| 50450015 | 2019.06.13 18:26:21 | buy | 0.01 | audcad_ecn | 0.91204 | 0.00000 | 0.00000 | 0.86296 | -0.10 | -0.42 | -14.93 |
| 50450029 | 2019.06.13 18:26:57 | sell | 0.01 | cadchf_ecn | 0.74574 | 0.00000 | 0.00000 | 0.75098 | -0.10 | -1.10 | -7.24 |
| 50450038 | 2019.06.13 18:27:02 | buy | 0.01 | cadchf_ecn | 0.74588 | 0.00000 | 0.00000 | 0.75283 | -0.10 | 3.46 | 6.97 |
| 50450043 | 2019.06.13 18:27:13 | sell | 0.01 | eurjpy_ecn | 119.771 | 3.00 | 3.00 | 117.847 | -0.10 | -1.28 | 17.81 |
| 50450046 | 2019.06.13 18:27:22 | buy | 0.01 | eurjpy_ecn | 119.769 | 3.00 | 3.00 | 117.848 | -0.10 | -3.56 | -17.82 |
| 50450047 | 2019.06.13 18:27:31 | sell | 0.01 | gbpchf_ecn | 1.23905 | 0.00000 | 0.00000 | 1.22727 | -0.10 | -1.59 | 3.74 |
| 50450050 | 2019.06.13 18:27:36 | buy | 0.01 | gbpchf_ecn | 1.23915 | 0.00000 | 0.00000 | 1.22717 | -0.10 | 5.22 | -4.10 |
| 50450055 | 2019.06.13 18:27:50 | sell | 0.01 | audchf_ecn | 0.68344 | 0.00000 | 0.00000 | 0.67242 | -0.10 | -3.97 | 8.09 |
| 50450059 | 2019.06.13 18:27:56 | buy | 0.01 | audchf_ecn | 0.68362 | 0.00000 | 0.00000 | 0.67229 | -0.10 | 5.28 | -8.16 |
| 50450066 | 2019.06.13 18:28:03 | sell | 0.01 | euraud_ecn | 1.60862 | 0.00000 | 0.00000 | 1.61729 | -0.10 | 3.56 | -5.71 |
| 50450071 | 2019.06.13 18:28:11 | buy | 0.01 | euraud_ecn | 1.60862 | 0.00000 | 0.00000 | 1.61696 | -0.10 | -4.13 | 5.49 |
| 50450075 | 2019.06.13 18:28:15 | sell | 0.01 | eurusd_ecn | 1.10792 | 0.00000 | 0.00000 | 1.09884 | -0.10 | 3.96 | 6.98 |
| 50450081 | 2019.06.13 18:28:26 | buy | 0.01 | eurusd_ecn | 1.10788 | 0.00000 | 0.00000 | 1.09880 | -0.10 | -4.99 | -17.08 |
| 50450085 | 2019.06.13 18:28:35 | sell | 0.01 | gbpnzd_ecn | 1.94942 | 0.00000 | 0.00000 | 1.96541 | -0.10 | -2.11 | -4.99 |
| 50450087 | 2019.06.13 18:28:41 | buy | 0.01 | gbpnzd_ecn | 1.94904 | 0.00000 | 0.00000 | 1.96595 | -0.10 | -1.26 | 9.85 |

Balance: 10 000.00 USD  Equity: 9 989.77  Free margin: 9 989.77 — -10.23

We Sell & Buy each currency at the same time, using 0.01 lot for each order.

After one or two hours, when the price have settled down in their own direction, we copy the currencies that are positive only. By using the currencies that are positive and leaving behind the negative ones, we increase our rate of success by diversifying our portfolio. We don't worry about the currencies that will eventually go negative at some point.

We are not actually letting any currency going full course into a target stop loss or take profit. We are waiting for the negatives and the positives to reach our overall profit target as input into our exit robot.

For note taking

# CHAPTER 5. CHARTS SET UP

We will set up 8 charts of the following currencies so that we can synchronize with the course. You may choose any currency that you prefer if you don't mind not being in synch with us.

AUDCAD, CADCHF, EURJPY, GBPCHF, AUDCHF, EURAUD, EURUSD, GBPNZD

And we will use the XAUUSD (Gold) for our exit robot so that we don't get confused with forex currencies when trading.

We chose the 8 currencies above in order to have a good diversity to trade with.

Here is a picture of the set up for your reference

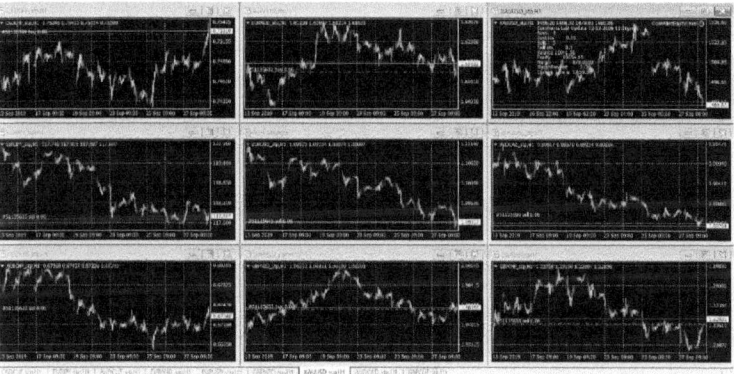

*The gold is the one on the top right and is our exit robot.*

For notes taking

# CHAPTER 6. TRADING WITH THE CALCULATOR

We use a professional trading calculator for 2 purposes. The first purpose is to calculate our number of lots, as we are funded by investors that enforce strict trading rules.

usdjpy

| | | USD | EUR |
|---|---|---|---|
| Stop Loss | 50 | | |
| Take Profit | 50 | | |
| Capital | | 10000 | 40000 |
| Risk % | | 2.000% | 0.250% |
| Money risked | | 200 | 100 |
| Profit expected | | 200 | 100 |
| **# of Lots** | | **0.426** | **0.237** |

The second purpose is to calculate the stop loss value, again a requirement enforced by the investors.

| | 5 Digit | 3 Digit |
|---|---|---|
| Entry Price | 1.75390 | 145.342 |
| Direction (B/S) | S | S |
| SL | 1.75890 | 145.842 |
| TP | 1.74890 | 144.842 |

For note taking

# Chapter 7. Setting Up the Exit robot

Our goal is to gain 10% per month on our capital. With a starting capital of $10000, we aim at a target of $1000. Because there are 20 trading days in a month, we would normally be trying to set up a target of $50 per day. But we don't know how long it will take us to get to our target, therefore we decided to set up our target at $100 per trading session. That enables us to keep orders open for 2 days. The exit robot is setup to cover this $100 gain on capital. See below the capital in account and the robot setup. The balance is $10152.35. The exit is set at 10165. There will be some slippage on exit while each order is being closed by the robot. So, we rounded the figure to $165 instead of $162.35

| 🗋 51165397 | | Common   Inputs | |
| 🗋 51165406 | | Variable | Value |
| ⊕ **Balance: 10 152.35 USD** | | 🔢 Equity Target | 10165 |
| | | 📄 CloseAllNow | false |

All the 8 open trades will be closed one after the other once the equity has reached $10165.

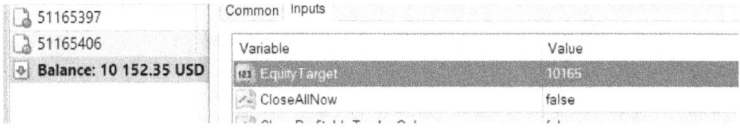

As soon as the robot has closed our trades with a $100 gain, we reset the platform by checking the experimental one and transferring the positive trades to the trading platform. We make sure that we reset the exit robot with an extra $100. If we forget, all trades will be closed at the same level that they were previously closed. This error means that we would be paying the costs with no gain at all.

For note taking

# Chapter 8. Setting up Analytics

For our analytics we use fxblue.com

To set this up we will need our MT4 trading account number and the investor password.

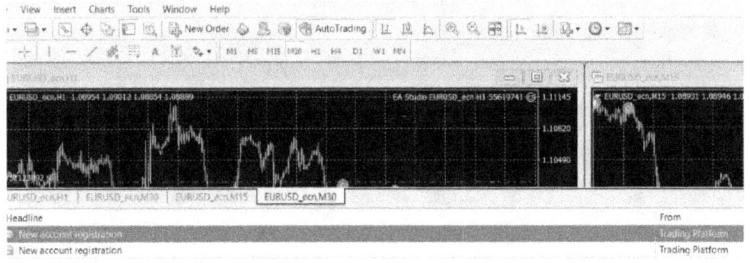

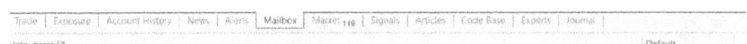

On the view tab, you select Terminal and then Mailbox. New account registration should appear. Double click on that and you will find the account number and the investor password that you will enter on the form in fxblue.

Open FXblue website and register your newly open account.

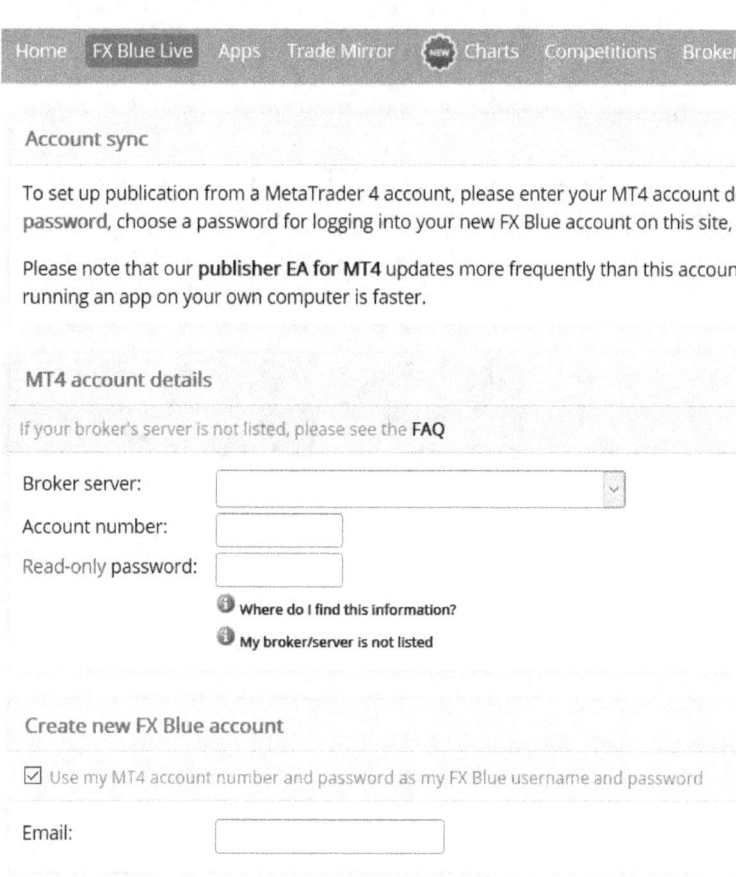

## Account sync

To set up publication from a MetaTrader 4 account, please enter your MT4 account de
password, choose a password for logging into your new FX Blue account on this site,

Please note that our **publisher EA for MT4** updates more frequently than this accoun
running an app on your own computer is faster.

### MT4 account details

If your broker's server is not listed, please see the **FAQ**

| | |
|---|---|
| Broker server: | |
| Account number: | |
| Read-only password: | |

 Where do I find this information?

 My broker/server is not listed

### Create new FX Blue account

☑ Use my MT4 account number and password as my FX Blue username and password

Email:

### Register

The read only password means the same thing as investor.
Don't use the trading password or the world will be able to
trade your account.

# CHAPTER 9. WHAT ANALYTICS?

## *Risk*

| Risk | |
|---|---|
| Risk/reward ratio: | 2.01 |
| Worst day: | 41.56 |
| Worst week: | 41.56 |
| Worst month: | 41.56 |
| Risk of ruin: | 0.0% |
| Trade length: | 3.6 days |
| Avg result: | +6.84 |
| Avg win: | +31.47 |
| Avg loss: | -22.26 |

We are looking at a risk reward ration RRR of 1:2 i.e. a reward twice the risk as it's the case on the above table.

We also want our average win to be superior to the average loss.

## *Stats*

| Stats | |
|---|---|
| Total return: | +1.6% |
| Monthly return: | +2.9% |
| Weekly return: | +0.7% |
| Peak drawdown: | - |
| Trade win %: | 54.2% |
| Profit factor: | 1.67 |
| Pips: | 304.8 |
| Trades per day: | 1.5 |
| History: | 16 days |

On this table, we are interested in the profit factor of at least 1.5 and a trade win >51%

# CHAPTER 7. CONCLUSION

This simple strategy brings us $100 per trading session often. It requires a bit of setup and patience but once understood and correctly prepared, it is an easy step into forex trading.

Happy Pips

# About The Author

"Paul Ardennes is an Author. He is working with various publishers including *Amazon* and *Barnes & Noble*.

He publishes courses on educational platforms such as *Udemy & Simpliv on **Spiritual Yoga and Forex trading***.

**He is a trained Electronic Medicine practitioner** (Scenar Cosmodic, Auricular therapy, Acupoints charting, electronic iris analysis, laser therapy and so on...), **an energy healer** (Seichim and Usui Reiki Master, informational medicine) **and a Forex researcher** (Algorithmic trading, fundamentals and technical fx trading).

He was introduced to Forex while researching yet another book. To cut a short story shorter, he got involved in forex competitions and started winning them and collecting money prizes.

That is when he discovered *Wall Street Investors' Club*, a private club where you enter by personal invitation only. They funded his trading skills.

His goal is to **impart stillness and silentness** within the emotional, turmoiled and turbulent minds of societies. He founded ***Spiritual Yoga*** to help with this ambition. Whether you join him to trade Forex for a second income or join him in the quest to inward peace and calm, the choice is there either way.

He is married to a Doctor gynaecologist and has 1 indigo son. They all live in Central America.

Join the parties. Join the Clubs"

*Amazon Editorial Vine Team Member*

# COURSES BY PAUL ARDENNES

### News release trading | FX Trading | Forex | Online Business

**NEW** 21 lectures • 1 hour • All Levels

Learn how to trade the news as a business | Online Business trading strategies | Use as a Hobby or business | fx trading | By **Paul Ardennes**

### London Open|Trade what bankers trade every morning | Forex

**NEW** 15 lectures • 38 mins • All Levels

The London Open trading system is the most popular fx trading strategy online |Unique Algorithmic trading system | | By **Paul Ardennes**

### Forex Trading| Algorithmic trading | Wall Street Investors

**NEW** 23 lectures • 1 hour • All Levels

FX Trading | Trading Forex with Trading Robots | The easy and smart way of trading the forex with algorithmic trading | By **Paul Ardennes**

# ONE LAST THING...

I would really appreciate your feedback to my books and courses. If you enjoyed them, can you gift me your best review marks so that they benefit other students?

If you found something that does not justify a good review, please, please let me know what exactly you want done or changed and I will make another video to reflect your views.

Happy Pips.

Paul Ardennes

Udemy course Instructor

www.ingramcontent.com/pod-product-compliance
Lightning Source LLC
Chambersburg PA
CBHW072240230526
45466CB00025B/2204